Dear Father

To:

....

From:

....

Date:

....

Dear Father

Weekly Devotionals
for Your Christian Journey

Nikka Santana

RESOURCE *Publications* · Eugene, Oregon

DEAR FATHER
Weekly Devotionals for Your Christian Journey

Resource Publications
An Imprint of Wipf and Stock Publishers
199 W. 8th Ave., Suite 3
Eugene, OR 97401

www.wipfandstock.com

PAPERBACK ISBN: 978-1-6667-1357-2
HARDCOVER ISBN: 978-1-6667-1358-9
EBOOK ISBN: 978-1-6667-1359-6

JULY 11, 2022 10:48 AM

Dedicated to all those who want to know GOD,
But don't know where to start the conversation.

Prayer is GOD's backstage pass into a personal audience with Him.

—DR. TONY EVANS

Contents

❧ Health & Wellness ❧

❧ GROWTH & DEVELOPMENT ❧

❧ RELATIONSHIPS ❧

Introduction

LIFE CAN BE COMPLEX and overwhelming, but GOD's love transcends all circumstances. He wants to elevate you in every facet of your being. All you must do is call on His name.

This book, alongside your Bible, will guide you through your year-long Christian journey. There is a different Bible verse presented for every week of the year, as well as a brief devotional to help you apply GOD's word. When you accompany these readings with a thorough study of the referenced passages, you will see significant improvement in your communion with the LORD.

Each week also presents a Time with GOD activity, which includes reflection questions, practices, and prompts to strengthen the understanding of your faith. Use this book as a space to cite your prayers, introspections, and revelations. Let your truth reign free.

Throughout this journey, allow yourself to be vulnerable with GOD. Step beyond your comfort zone. Indulge in His presence. Like all relationships, this bond requires time and communication. At the end of the year, you will be glad to reflect on your spiritual growth!

&ى Faith &ى

Week 1: Seeking GOD

And when you and your children return to the LORD your GOD
and obey him with all your heart and with all your soul according
to everything I command you today, then the LORD your GOD will
restore your fortunes and have compassion on you and gather you
again from all the nations where he scattered you.

DEUTERONOMY 30:2–3, NIV

Dear Father,

I turn to You in all humility to strengthen Our relationship. Forgive me if I have ever allowed any distractions to come above my
faith. Take the broken pieces of me and make me whole.

LORD, I pray for Your mercy and guidance as I center my life
around You. I cannot navigate this world on my own, without Your
direction.

I will come to You in good times and in bad. You are above all else,
and You complete me. I pray to feel Your warm embrace around
me, for my commitment to You is complete and shall never be
compromised.

Amen.

Time with GOD

When was the last time you felt distant from GOD? What made it difficult to prioritize your faith?

....

....

....

....

....

....

....

....

....

....

....

....

....

....

Week 2: The LORD's Word

All Scripture is GOD-breathed and is useful for teaching, rebuking, correcting and training in righteousness, so that the servant of GOD may be thoroughly equipped for every good work.

2 TIMOTHY 3:16–17, NIV

Dear Father,

The Bible carries great power by making Your word so accessible. Allow me to fully utilize this gift. May I grasp Your teachings with sound acceptance and stay grounded in Your supernatural ways.

Allow sermons and addresses to awaken me to Your truth. Help me to acknowledge these implications in my life so that I can walk according to Your will. The Bible is alive, and I pray to experience its greatness.

My heart, mind, and soul are open and ready for You. Speak to me and teach me, LORD, for I am eager to be armed by Your word. May the gospel light up the world and continue to bond Your children together as we lead our lives of faith.

Amen.

Time with GOD

What Bible verses do you find most inspiring? Write them down on sticky notes and post them around your house. Allow them to remind you that GOD is always present.

....

....

....

....

....

....

....

....

....

....

....

....

....

Week 3: Trust

Trust in the LORD with all your heart and lean not on your own understanding; in all your ways submit to him, and he will make your paths straight.

PROVERBS 3:5–6, NIV

Dear Father,

I stand firm in my faith, for You are always at work. I lean not on my own strength, but on Your power, which moves even the greatest of mountains.

I release my control to You as I hand over the weight of my fears and uncertainties. I embrace every season because I am taken care of. You are above all earthly things, and You shield me from harm.

May my confidence serve as a testimony of Your unwavering glory.

Amen.

Time with GOD

Reflect on a time of uncertainty. How did GOD resolve the situation in the end?

....

....

....

....

....

....

....

....

....

....

....

....

....

Week 4: GOD's Sovereignty

For the LORD is our judge, the LORD is our lawgiver, the LORD is
our king; it is he who will save us.

ISAIAH 33:22, NIV

Dear Father,

You are the creator of all things, seen and unseen. You alone reign
over heaven and earth.

Even in light of blessings and abundance, may I live a life of humility. Remind me that You can recall Your endowments just as
easily as You have gifted them. I am nothing in comparison to Your
power; I am at Your mercy.

Thank You, LORD, for favoring me, even when I am undeserving.
My successes and accomplishments are not mine to claim; rather,
they are the result of Your generous works. I call on Your name to
praise You and glorify You!

Amen.

Time with GOD

Close your eyes and take a moment to envision the kingdom of heaven. What do you see? What do you hear? How does it make you feel?

....

....

....

....

....

....

....

....

....

....

....

....

Week 5: Provision

Look at the birds of the air: they neither sow nor reap nor gather into barns, and yet your heavenly Father feeds them. Are you not of more value than they?

MATTHEW 6:26, ESV

Dear Father,

You nourish, You provide, and You deliver! From my necessities to my riches, I am always taken care of. I relinquish my worries as I place full confidence in Your divine provision.

I need not stress about the future, nor harbor doubt in my spirit. Everything that I have is in accordance with Your will. Everything that is meant for me will be granted, for You have promised fullness and abundance.

Today, I commit to living in the present and rejoicing in Your everlasting love.

Amen.

Time with GOD

This week, go for a peaceful walk through nature. Look around and observe all of GOD's creations. What calls you to believe in the gospel?

....

....

....

....

....

....

....

....

....

....

....

....

Week 6: Repentance of Sins

He has not dealt with us according to our sins, Nor punished us according to our iniquities. For as the heavens are high above the earth, So great is His mercy toward those who fear Him; As far as the east is from the west, So far has He removed our transgressions from us. As a father pities his children, So the LORD pities those who fear Him. For He knows our frame; He remembers that we are dust.

PSALM 103:10-14, NKJV

Dear Father,

I bow down to You to confess my sins. I will not hide nor deny my imperfections, for You alone can lift the darkness within me. As I bear all and reflect, I thank You for the gift of salvation.

May You hear my cries and forgive me for my wrongdoings. I lean on Your guidance as I commit to a more fruitful life.

Wash away my sins, LORD, and allow me to start over. Release me from the shackles of regret, and help me to learn from my mistakes instead. May I move forth with a renewed spirit.

Amen.

Time with GOD

Find some quiet time to examine your heart and reflect on your sins. Then, close your eyes and ask GOD for His forgiveness and direction.

....

....

....

....

....

....

....

....

....

....

....

....

....

Week 7: Accountability

Brothers and sisters, if someone is caught in a sin, you who live by the Spirit should restore that person gently. But watch yourselves, or you also may be tempted. Carry each other's burdens, and in this way you will fulfill the law of Christ.

GALATIANS 6:1–2, NIV

Dear Father,

Teach me the way of righteousness and guide me with Your Holy Spirit. I assume full responsibility for my past mistakes as I commit to a renewed life of good virtue.

I pray for the courage to correct my actions, and I pray for the restoration of those that I have hurt. Help me to be better in my relationships with others and with You, GOD.

Use me to hold my brothers and sisters accountable when they fail to live by Your will. May I resist temptation, and instead have the courage to redirect those in need. We are all Your children, LORD, so we shall all be uplifted in unity.

Amen.

Time with GOD

In what ways can you become a better Christian? What is GOD calling you to change?

....

....

....

....

....

....

....

....

....

....

....

....

....

Week 8: Reflection

Examine yourselves to see whether you are in the faith; test yourselves. Do you not realize that Christ Jesus is in you—unless, of course, you fail the test?

2 CORINTHIANS 13:5, NIV

Dear Father,

As I take the time to be still and reflect, help me to examine the intentions of my heart. Allow me to step away from the world's noise and seek clarity of mind.

Show me what I have done right today, and show me what I can improve. Awaken me to the things that I have overlooked, and uncover any self-seeking motives that may linger.

I pray to learn from my evaluations, while still maintaining a gentle and self-affirming tone with myself. I will continue to try my hardest, for I am sculpted by Your lessons.

Amen.

Time with GOD

When you ask GOD for answers, do you ever take a moment to listen? What are some revelations that He has brought you to?

....

....

....

....

....

....

....

....

....

....

....

....

....

....

Week 9: Gifts & Talents

Each of you should use whatever gift you have received to serve others, as faithful stewards of GOD's grace in its various forms. If anyone speaks, they should do so as one who speaks the very words of GOD. If anyone serves, they should do so with the strength GOD provides, so that in all things GOD may be praised through Jesus Christ. To him be the glory and the power for ever and ever. Amen.

1 PETER 4:10−11, NIV

Dear Father,

I acknowledge that my gifts are not for me to exploit for my own benefit, but to glorify You with. May I align these strengths with Your teachings, LORD, so that I can discover my unique role in making this world a better place.

All work that I do is in Your name, Father, and I pray that You administer me. I will channel these talents to serve my brothers and sisters, as I have been created to do.

I am waiting with an open heart and an open mind for Your direction. Just say the word, and I shall commit.

Amen.

Time with GOD

What are your unique gifts and strengths? How are you using them to serve others?

....

....

....

....

....

....

....

....

....

....

....

....

....

....

Week 10: Worldly Temptations

Do not be conformed to this world, but be transformed by the renewal of your mind, that by testing you may discern what is the will of GOD, what is good and acceptable and perfect.

ROMANS 12:2, ESV

Dear Father,

Forgive me if I have ever neglected my faith in pursuit of worldly riches or acceptance. Help me to keep an eternal perspective as I define my values. You alone are the Almighty, whose sole approval shall dictate my lifestyle.

Prepare my heart to resist temptation, and keep me from any situations that may derail me. Help me to release my desires for anything that does not serve You.

Your glory surpasses all temporary pleasures. Thank You for being everything that I need and more.

Amen.

Time with GOD

What is one of your bad habits? Set a realistic goal to cut back on that habit this week. Call on GOD for His guidance as you commit to this challenge.

....

....

....

....

....

....

....

....

....

....

....

....

....

Week 11: Spiritual Battles

Be alert and of sober mind. Your enemy the devil prowls around like a roaring lion looking for someone to devour. Resist him, standing firm in the faith, because you know that the family of believers throughout the world is undergoing the same kind of sufferings.

1 PETER 5:8–9, NIV

Dear Father,

Have mercy on me if I have ever questioned Your greatness. In the face of adversity and seemingly unanswered prayers, I may sometimes forget that You are good all the time.

When worldly logic fails me, enlighten me, LORD. Remind me that You have Your hands on every situation, even in moments of hardship. Your divine plans are meant to be beyond my understanding, so I will not settle for the devil's easy bait.

If I shall ever fall uncertain again, I pray to quickly overcome the internal battle. You alone are the light, and I shall always be fully confident in Your will.

Amen.

Time with GOD

List ten ways that GOD is actively working in your life.

....

....

....

....

....

....

....

....

....

....

....

....

....

....

....

Week 12: Power of the Tongue

The tongue has the power of life and death,
and those who love it will eat its fruit.

PROVERBS 18:21, NIV

Dear Father,

May my faith always be reflected in the choice of my words and expressions.

Guide my mouth as I speak, and help me in becoming Your ideal messenger. Purify my intentions, and keep me from the temptations of lies, gossip, and slander.

With the gospel in my heart, I pray to always use my words for good. I seek to uplift others and share Your divine light through my speech.

Amen.

Time with GOD

Words carry great influence. This week, be mindful of your speech—avoid gossiping, complaining, and using foul language. At the end of the week, reflect on how this has shifted your perceptions.

....

....

....

....

....

....

....

....

....

....

....

....

....

Week 13: Joy

You will go out in joy and be led forth in peace; the mountains and hills will burst into song before you, and all the trees of the field will clap their hands.

ISAIAH 55:12, NIV

Dear Father,

I praise You and glorify You for all that You do! I exalt Your name in celebration, for Your works are insurmountable. You are the enabler who owes us nothing, yet gives us everything.

Through my worship, I seek to share Your light with my brothers and sisters. We lift up our hearts to You, GOD.

Thank You for Your unconditional favor!

Amen.

Time with GOD

Remember that you are blessed and highly favored by the LORD! This week, begin every morning by giving glory to GOD. Before checking your phone or turning on the TV, journal about three things that you are grateful for.

....

....

....

....

....

....

....

....

....

....

....

....

....

HEALTH & WELLNESS

Week 14: Inner Healing

Call to me and I will answer you, and will tell you great and hidden
things that you have not known.

JEREMIAH 33:3, ESV

Dear Father,

While I may sometimes dwell on the past, I know that all trials are
lessons from You. I am stronger, and I am wiser. My pains do not
define me.

Through Your glory, I have been lifted and renewed. This is my
exodus, and as I transition into a greater version of myself, I ask
that You grant me healing for my internal battles.

Please, GOD, hear the prayers that I cannot form into words,
for You alone know my deepest sorrows. May You be the light
throughout my healing journey.

Amen.

Time with GOD

What inner conflicts are you facing? Bear it all to the LORD. Allow yourself to cry to Him if you need to. He is listening, and He wants to lift your pains.

....

....

....

....

....

....

....

....

....

....

....

....

....

....

Week 15: Physical Wellness

For he will command his angels concerning you to guard you in all your ways; they will lift you up in their hands, so that you will not strike your foot against a stone.

PSALM 91:11–12, NIV

Dear Father,

Thank You for Your heavenly protection. You look out for me in ways beyond my awareness.

I am blessed with a body that is nurtured and able. You shield me from illness, injury, and mishap. You are the Mighty Healer who closes all wounds and soothes all pains.

LORD, I seek refuge in You, for You keep me safe.

Amen.

Time with GOD

Set aside ten minutes each morning to stretch your body. As you do so, be mindful of your movements and thank GOD for all of your physical capabilities.

....

....

....

....

....

....

....

....

....

....

....

....

....

Week 16: A Blessed Home

Through wisdom a house is built, And by understanding it is established; By knowledge the rooms are filled With all precious and pleasant riches.

PROVERBS 24:3–4, NKJV

Dear Father,

I welcome You fondly into my home. Bless this house, LORD, and fill each room with Your presence. May every soul that enters experience the warmth of Your love.

Allow this to be a place of peace and restoration. Protect it from all harm, both physically and spiritually.

I reside soundly within these walls, knowing that I am guarded by the Almighty King.

Amen.

Time with GOD

Take a walk around your house and reflect on the times that you have felt GOD's presence in each room. What was the occasion? How did it go?

....

....

....

....

....

....

....

....

....

....

....

....

....

Week 17: Feeding the Soul

For the grace of GOD has appeared, bringing salvation for all people, training us to renounce ungodliness and worldly passions, and to live self-controlled, upright, and godly lives in the present age.

TITUS 2:11–12, ESV

Dear Father,

I pray that You guide me in choosing the content I consume, from the films I watch to the music I listen to.

Lend me the wisdom to rise above any harmful media or trends, and keep me from the desire for worldly validation.

I shall remain grounded in my faith by properly feeding my soul. You speak to me through many mediums, LORD, and I am eager to welcome You in.

Amen.

Time with GOD

Create a playlist of your favorite gospel music. Then, listen to it in the car or while you run your errands throughout the week.

Take the time to dissect and comprehend the lyrics. How do they apply to your life?

....

....

....

....

....

....

....

....

....

....

....

....

Week 18: Slow to Anger

Know this, my beloved brothers: let every person be quick to hear, slow to speak, slow to anger; for the anger of man does not produce the righteousness of GOD.

JAMES 1:19-20, ESV

Dear Father,

When I grow angry, my spirit is weak and vulnerable. If I am ever tempted to respond out of rage, I pray that You keep me grounded in my faith.

Place Your hand on my shoulder and guide me to express myself according to Your will. Help me to pause and assess before reacting.

LORD, I lean on You to gain peace and clarity. Help me to be more like You, for You are perfect in all ways.

Amen.

Time with GOD

Set aside a moment each day to practice deep breathing: Inhale for four seconds, hold your breath for four seconds, then exhale for four seconds. Repeat this process for about a minute each time. As you do this exercise, feel GOD's peace filling your spirit. Invite Him into your mind and body.

....

....

....

....

....

....

....

....

....

....

....

....

Week 19: Straying from Judgment

Brothers and sisters, do not slander one another. Anyone who speaks against a brother or sister or judges them speaks against the law and judges it. When you judge the law, you are not keeping it, but sitting in judgment on it. There is only one Lawgiver and Judge, the one who is able to save and destroy. But you—who are you to judge your neighbor?

JAMES 4:11–12, NIV

Dear Father,

As I seek to overcome my judgmental nature, I come to You for counsel.

May You grant me a heart of understanding, and not of criticism. Help me not to condemn, but to serve.

I pray to embrace everyone's differences and unique walks of life, for I am reminded of my unity with all those around me.

Amen.

Time with GOD

Try a new activity this week, like joining a class or attending an event. Push yourself to step out of your comfort zone.

Afterward, have a conversation with GOD. What did you enjoy about the experience?

....

....

....

....

....

....

....

....

....

....

....

....

....

Week 20: Fight against Depression

When the righteous cry for help, the LORD hears and delivers them
out of all their troubles. The LORD is near to the brokenhearted and
saves the crushed in spirit.

PSALM 34:17–18, ESV

Dear Father,

When my sorrows take over my mind, please be the guiding force
that works through me. Restore my spirit and speak to me, LORD.
Navigate me through these challenging times.

May You open my eyes to any harmful circumstances and grant
me the courage to remove myself. Lead me to the right resources
so that I can recover.

I depend on Your light in the darkness. Thank You for being my
strength as I pray for a better tomorrow.

Amen.

Time with GOD

Sometimes, depression is a call for change. Think about what changes you need right now. Bring your requests to GOD, and ask for clarity and guidance.

....

....

....

....

....

....

....

....

....

....

....

....

Week 21: Overcoming Anxiety

For GOD has not given us a spirit of fear,
but of power and of love and of a sound mind.

2 TIMOTHY 1:7, NKJV

Dear Father,

When I am overwhelmed with panic and anxiety, I turn to You for comfort. I know that You are always ready to lift my burdens.

LORD, remind me of Your unwavering power and clear my mind of these unsettling thoughts. Help me to stay grounded in my present and physical being.

Thank You for always watching over me and guarding me against all dangers.

Amen.

Time with GOD

Take a moment to relax—pause, unclench your jaw, and loosen your shoulders. Remember that GOD is always in control.

Make a list of all of your worries. Then, ask GOD to lift them from you by praying about each item one at a time.

....

....

....

....

....

....

....

....

....

....

....

....

Week 22: Power of Prayer

Therefore I tell you, whatever you ask in prayer, believe that you have received it, and it will be yours.

MARK 11:24, ESV

Dear Father,

When I find myself longing for answers and direction, I come to You in prayer. You are my outlet as I pour the contents of my soul.

LORD, our relationship is like no other. You know me in my truest form; You live within me. Provide me with the clarity that I cannot find in earthly things.

Bless me with revelations and a change of heart. May my prayers bring me peace and clarity, for the words that we share hold immense power.

Amen.

Time with GOD

Do you have some downtime on your daily commute? Don't turn on your music right away. Instead, make travel time a time of prayer. Talk to GOD and share everything that's on your mind. Feel His presence wherever you go.

....

....

....

....

....

....

....

....

....

....

....

....

....

Week 23: Treating My Temple

Do you not know that your bodies are temples of the Holy Spirit, who is in you, whom you have received from GOD? You are not your own; you were bought at a price. Therefore honor GOD with your bodies.

1 CORINTHIANS 6:19–20, NIV

Dear Father,

I know that my body is Yours and not my own. It serves to house my spirit, so I shall handle it with great care.

May You nourish the food that I eat and help me to stay active. Guide me in choosing what I allow into my temple, and grant me self-control and consistency.

I seek to form healthy routines, not out of insecurity or self-loathing, but out of love. I shall praise You through the way that I treat my body.

Amen.

Time with GOD

Commit to at least thirty minutes of physical activity every day this week. Before each session, repeat the following affirmation: I am blessed to be strong and healthy, so I dedicate this workout to GOD.

....

....

....

....

....

....

....

....

....

....

....

....

Week 24: Rest

Come to me, all you who are weary and burdened,
and I will give you rest.

MATTHEW 11:28, NIV

Dear Father,

As I step away from my regular responsibilities, I pray to receive the rest that I need. I lay all of my agendas and worries at Your feet, for You are my safe haven when I am overworked.

Thank You for granting me the time to ease my mind and re-center my spirit. Replenish me in all the ways that I need. In my relaxation, I meditate on Your word and find serenity in Your provision.

When I return to my normal schedules, may I be blessed with renewed positivity and a heart of optimism. Thank You for Your sacred touch.

Amen.

Time with GOD

Set aside ten minutes each day this week to practice stillness. Quiet your thoughts and emotions, and repeat the mantra: GOD has me covered.

....

....

....

....

....

....

....

....

....

....

....

....

....

Week 25: Self-Control

No temptation has overtaken you except what is common to
mankind. And GOD is faithful; he will not let you be tempted beyond
what you can bear. But when you are tempted, he will also provide a
way out so that you can endure it.

1 CORINTHIANS 10:13, NIV

Dear Father,

Whenever I am fighting temptation, I turn to You for guidance. By
Your will, I shall rise above my weaknesses and addictions.

In my commitment to You, I have gained strength and self-control.
You are superior to any of the devil's schemes, and You will keep
me on the path of righteousness.

Thank You for empowering me throughout my course.

Amen.

Time with GOD

What temptations are you currently facing? Call on GOD for His guidance as you seek to overcome them.

....

....

....

....

....

....

....

....

....

....

....

....

....

....

Week 26: Healing of Others

Is anyone among you sick? Let him call for the elders of the church, and let them pray over him, anointing him with oil in the name of the LORD. And the prayer of faith will save the sick, and the LORD will raise him up. And if he has committed sins, he will be forgiven.

JAMES 5:14–15, NKJV

Dear Father,

In Your name, I speak healing over all those who are suffering. I pray for them to experience a quick recovery, whether physically or emotionally.

You alone can banish the illnesses, pains, and sorrows that burden Your people. May You grant them good health and prosperity.

Lead them to seek refuge in You, LORD. Allow them to release their worries and be uplifted by the breadth of Your love.

Amen.

Time with GOD

Do you know anyone who's going through a tough time right now?
Reach out to them this week and offer words of support.

Then, in your daily prayers, ask GOD to grant them strength and
healing.

....

....

....

....

....

....

....

....

....

....

....

....

GROWTH & DEVELOPMENT

Week 27: Self-Improvement

Therefore, if anyone is in Christ, he is a new creation. The old has passed away; behold, the new has come.

2 CORINTHIANS 5:17, ESV

Dear Father,

As I take the time to better myself, I pray that You help me to identify my weaknesses and shortcomings. Today, I begin my journey of molding myself into Your ideal servant.

I call on You to be my source of discipline and guidance. Help me to embrace the things I cannot change, while working on the things that I can.

GOD, please be with me as I take every step. With Your Spirit poured into me, I am confident in my pursuit of growth.

Amen.

Time with GOD

Look through an old photo album and reflect on how GOD was present in different stages of your life.

What experiences did He provide? What people did He work through? How much have you grown?

....

....

....

....

....

....

....

....

....

....

....

....

Week 28: Trials & Tribulations

I have said these things to you, that in me you may have peace. In the world you will have tribulation. But take heart; I have overcome the world.

JOHN 16:33, ESV

Dear Father,

When failure and misfortune leave me feeling hopeless, I pray that You lift my gaze. May I be steadfast and determined as I maneuver the course set before me. No obstacle can compare to Your greatness.

Remind me that You have already won my battles for me. I operate in the power of the Holy Spirit; therefore, I can never lose sight of my goals.

GOD, allow these tests to develop me so that I can grow in my faith. I shall find peace in every circumstance, for I know that, as Your child, I will always succeed in the end.

Amen.

Time with GOD

What conflicts have you overcome? What lessons did GOD teach
you through those experiences?

....

....

....

....

....

....

....

....

....

....

....

....

....

Week 29: Inspiration & Motivation

You will eat the fruit of your labor; blessings and prosperity will be
yours.

PSALM 128:2, NIV

Dear Father,

You are intentional with what You speak into my heart. So if You
have called me to do work, I know that I am equipped for it.

Everything that I dream of is already mine; it is simply waiting for
me on the other side. With Your favor, it is not a matter of "if," but
"when."

LORD, cleanse my spirit of laziness and procrastination. If I am in-
spired to do something, help me to take action. Whether they are
personal or professional goals, I pray that You push me to achieve
my full potential.

Amen.

Time with GOD

What is a goal that you are working toward? Pray as if you have already accomplished it. Envision it and believe it. Thank GOD for His favor and goodness.

....

....

....

....

....

....

....

....

....

....

....

....

....

....

Week 30: Self-Love

For you created my inmost being; you knit me together in my
mother's womb. I praise you because I am fearfully and wonderfully
made; your works are wonderful, I know that full well.

PSALM 139:13–14, NIV

Dear Father,

I am wonderfully and uniquely made, for I am graced by Your
touch. From my image to my soul, I am sculpted to perfection.

I take the time today to appreciate my every feature and my every
ability. With Your endowments, I am limitless; I am unstoppable.

You are meticulous in all of Your works, and for that, I am truly
blessed.

Amen.

Time with GOD

Celebrate yourself this week. Get dressed up and take yourself out on a date. Treat yourself to the things you like.

Then, reflect on the ways that GOD has created you in His image.

....

....

....

....

....

....

....

....

....

....

....

....

....

....

Week 31: Peace with the Past

Brothers and sisters, I do not consider myself yet to have taken hold
of it. But one thing I do: Forgetting what is behind and straining
toward what is ahead, I press on toward the goal to win the prize for
which GOD has called me heavenward in Christ Jesus.

PHILIPPIANS 3:13–14, NIV

Dear Father,

I come before You to submit to You. Grant me the serenity to release my past and accept the things that cannot be undone.

Renew my spirit; heal me from my traumas. Help me to forgive
both myself and others.

All of my experiences have shaped me into who am I today. I graciously accept my lessons and move forth with the strength that I
have gained. In this moment, I am choosing to let go.

Amen.

Time with GOD

Have you ever hurt others because you were hurt? If so, talk to GOD about your experiences. Ask Him for the strength to truly let go of your pain.

....

....

....

....

....

....

....

....

....

....

....

....

....

Week 32: Opportunities

And whatever you do, whether in word or deed, do it all in the name
of the LORD Jesus, giving thanks to GOD the Father through him.

COLOSSIANS 3:17, NIV

Dear Father,

I am so grateful for the opportunities that You have aligned for me.
You remove all limits to my success and continue to elevate me.

Thank You for opening all the right doors and closing the wrong
ones too. You have protected me from what I once wanted so that
You could provide me with what I truly needed.

I walk fully in Your blessings and goodness. All praise to the Most
High, for my GOD always delivers!

Amen.

Time with GOD

Write about a time that GOD answered your prayers.

....

....

....

....

....

....

....

....

....

....

....

....

....

....

Week 33: GOD's Divine Timing

For I know the plans I have for you, declares the LORD, plans for welfare and not for evil, to give you a future and a hope. Then you will call upon me and come and pray to me, and I will hear you.

JEREMIAH 29:11-12, ESV

Dear Father,

Fill me with Your spirit of patience and assurance. May I foster these virtues as I grow in every area of my life.

When my plans are not fulfilled, help me find peace in Your intention. I shall take each obstacle as a necessary lesson and redirection. You see further down the road than I can, LORD, and so I place my trust in You.

In overcoming conflict, I release my expectations and embrace my journey instead. May I be reminded that all things are in accordance with Your timing.

Amen.

Time with GOD

In what ways does GOD show patience toward you?

....

....

....

....

....

....

....

....

....

....

....

....

....

....

Week 34: New Journey

Have I not commanded you? Be strong and courageous. Do not be afraid; do not be discouraged, for the LORD your GOD will be with you wherever you go.

JOSHUA 1:9, NIV

Dear Father,

For every new journey that I begin, I turn to You for counsel and fortitude. While the future may sometimes be unclear, I am granted the strength to walk fearlessly into every chapter of my life.

With my trust in You, LORD, I embrace change and new beginnings. Even when I wander far from familiarity, You are always by my side.

I know that You are preparing to elevate me, and I am eager to accept Your blessings.

Amen.

Time with GOD

Are you preparing to start a new journey? Perhaps you're starting a new school year or training for a new job.

Write a letter to your future self: Speak about your feelings regarding this transition, ask yourself questions, and offer prayers. Then, keep the letter in a safe place until you're ready to revisit it, whether it's a few months or a few years down the road.

....

....

....

....

....

....

....

....

....

....

....

....

Week 35: Fulfilling My Purpose

For we are His workmanship, created in Christ Jesus for good works,
which GOD prepared beforehand that we should walk in them.

EPHESIANS 2:10, NKJV

Dear Father,

Help me to live fully in my purpose. In surrendering my life to
You, I pray that You reveal my appointed mission. I seek to praise
You and glorify You through my works.

I invite Your Spirit to take control. Help me discover what captures
my heart and sparks my determination. You have created me with
such drive, and I pray to use it for good.

Place me in the right environment to make an impact, and provide
me the opportunities to serve. LORD, any platform that I am given
will be used to worship You.

Amen.

Time with GOD

What are Your biggest dreams? Don't be ashamed to express their full grandeur to GOD. Write out every detail exactly as you envision it.

....

....

....

....

....

....

....

....

....

....

....

....

....

Week 36: Confidence

I can do all things through Christ who strengthens me.

PHILIPPIANS 4:13, NKJV

Dear Father,

I hold my head high, knowing that You have invested Your-self in me. I exude poise because I am aware of my overflowing abundance.

GOD of all love, You are my source of confidence. May I walk into every situation knowing that You have sent me; May I take up space with full intention; And may I communicate with certainty and conviction. I will never allow myself to feel small with a spirit so big.

You erase my doubts and insecurities. With Your favor, I have trust in myself. I am ready to get out of my head and step into my worth.

Amen.

Time with GOD

Write about a time that you felt confident and accomplished. How did GOD play a role in this experience?

....

....

....

....

....

....

....

....

....

....

....

....

....

....

Week 37: Strength Against Enemies

Put on the full armor of GOD, so that you can take your stand against the devil's schemes. For our struggle is not against flesh and blood, but against the rulers, against the authorities, against the powers of this dark world and against the spiritual forces of evil in the heavenly realms.

EPHESIANS 6:11–12, NIV

Dear Father,

Grant me the strength to stand firm against my enemies. I equip myself with Your armor, for my battles are fierce and spiritual.

May You remind me that my fight is not against people nor objects, but against the true opponent, which is sin. Save me from my selfish, fallen nature, and help me to combat the devil's attacks.

You are my fortitude in the face of adversity, and with You, I will prevail. I seek comfort in knowing that I am placed only in situations that I can overcome.

Amen.

Time with GOD

Reflect on the armor of GOD, one piece at a time. Which virtues are most important to you and why?

....

....

....

....

....

....

....

....

....

....

....

....

....

Week 38: Financial Security

The LORD will grant you abundant prosperity—in the fruit of your womb, the young of your livestock and the crops of your ground—in the land he swore to your ancestors to give you. The LORD will open the heavens, the storehouse of his bounty, to send rain on your land in season and to bless all the work of your hands. You will lend to many nations but will borrow from none.

DEUTERONOMY 28:11–12, NIV

Dear Father,

I glorify You for Your physical and economic provision. You have never failed to deliver me.

Thank You, GOD, for enabling my financial blessings. May You continue to align me with the right opportunities so that I can support myself and my loved ones.

I believe in Your plan, and I seek comfort in knowing that You wish wealth upon Your people.

Amen.

Time with GOD

What financial opportunities has GOD aligned for you? What opportunities are you seeking next?

....

....

....

....

....

....

....

....

....

....

....

....

....

Week 39: Balance

To everything there is a season, A time for every purpose under heaven:

ECCLESIASTES 3:1, NKJV

Dear Father,

In a world so consumed by success and merit, help me to slow down when my daily endeavors get ahead of my faith. Guide me in achieving a fruitful, balanced life that revolves around You, LORD.

May I tend equally to all of my callings. I seek to uphold my relationships with fullness and passion; I seek to care for myself and all of my needs; And I seek to enjoy every moment of Your light and blessings.

As I assess the different areas of my life, grant me the wisdom to see what is out of line. Direct me in prioritizing what is important, and provide me the awareness to step away from the things that are overdone.

Amen.

Time with GOD

What are your priorities in life? Take a moment to pray about each one, then ask GOD to help you maintain a healthy balance.

....

....

....

....

....

....

....

....

....

....

....

....

....

....

RELATIONSHIPS

Week 40: Family

No one has ever seen GOD; if we love one another, GOD abides in us
and his love is perfected in us.

1 JOHN 4:12, ESV

Dear Father,

I am so thankful for my beloved family. We are graciously covered
by Your wings. Please continue to watch over us, and grant us good
health and harmony.

I pray for each of us individually and as a whole. May You hear our
petitions and provide us with our silent needs.

It is truly a blessing to be unified and guided by You, our heavenly
King.

Amen.

Time with GOD

Sometimes we don't express our love enough. This week, make it a point to tell each of your closest family members that you love them. Let them know how much they mean to you.

....

....

....

....

....

....

....

....

....

....

....

....

....

Week 41: Choosing Relationships

May the GOD of endurance and encouragement grant you to live
in such harmony with one another, in accord with Christ Jesus, that
together you may with one voice glorify the GOD and Father of our
LORD Jesus Christ.

ROMANS 15:5-6, ESV

Dear Father,

May the relationships that I welcome into my life be genuine and
pure. Lead me to people who encourage me to walk in faith. Allow
us to uplift one another.

Should anyone lead me astray, I ask that You grant me the courage
to remove myself from their company. Protect me from any ill-
intentioned spirits, and guard my peace and fruitfulness.

I place my trust in You as I seek to nurture meaningful friendships
and bonds.

Amen.

Time with GOD

Who are your closest friends? In what ways have you helped each other grow in faith?

Reach out to each of them this week and ask them how you can pray for them.

....

....

....

....

....

....

....

....

....

....

....

....

....

Week 42: Romantic Love

Love is patient, love is kind. It does not envy, it does not boast, it is not proud. It does not dishonor others, it is not self-seeking, it is not easily angered, it keeps no record of wrongs. Love does not delight in evil but rejoices with the truth. It always protects, always trusts, always hopes, always perseveres.

1 CORINTHIANS 13:4–7, NIV

Dear Father,

I pray for my partner and me to experience Your love and divine grace in our relationship. May we uphold integrity in times of temptation, perseverance in times of hardship, and companionship as we grow. Our faith in You shall always remain the core of our bond.

I submit to You, LORD, so that I can be the best version of myself for my partner. I commit to loving them with the purity and passion that You have intended.

May You serve as our light throughout our lives together, for a relationship that truly welcomes the Holy Spirit can never fail.

Amen.

Time with GOD

With your partner, find a Bible scripture that is relevant in your lives. Take the week to reflect on it and memorize it together.

....

....

....

....

....

....

....

....

....

....

....

....

....

....

Week 43: Healthy Boundaries

Do not be deceived: "Bad company ruins good morals."

1 CORINTHIANS 15:33, ESV

Dear Father,

Guard me against all ill intentions, whether seen or unseen. Keep me from accepting any form of mistreatment, and grant me the wisdom to set boundaries when necessary.

I pray that You navigate me in handling any harmful relationships. Remind me of my worth, for I am a child of the Almighty King.

May I have the compassion to forgive those who have hurt me, while also maintaining the self-respect to protect my spirit.

Amen.

Time with GOD

Do you need to set boundaries with anyone in your life? Lay your troubles before the LORD and ask for the courage to make a change.

....

....

....

....

....

....

....

....

....

....

....

....

....

....

Week 44: Forgiveness

You shall not take vengeance, nor bear any grudge against the children of your people, but you shall love your neighbor as yourself: I am the LORD.

LEVITICUS 19:18, NKJV

Dear Father,

Lead me to forgive, even when it is hard. Heal my soul, and help me to empathize with those who have hurt me.

If I have sinned against any of my brothers and sisters, I pray for the courage to acknowledge my faults and to seek compassion as well. May we learn to dismiss resentment, for we are all Your children, even in the face of disagreement.

My mouth shall only speak words of love and positivity, LORD. I commit to forgiving others so that I can worship You with every ounce of my being.

Amen.

Time with GOD

Are you holding any grudges? Ask GOD for the strength to forgive, then take the time to pray for those who have hurt you.

....

....

....

....

....

....

....

....

....

....

....

....

....

....

Week 45: Coping with Loneliness

Fear not, for I am with you; be not dismayed, for I am your GOD;
I will strengthen you, I will help you, I will uphold you with my
righteous right hand.

ISAIAH 41:10, ESV

Dear Father,

When I feel lonely, I turn to You. Even when there is no one else
to confide in, I know that You are always here to listen to my cries.

May I use these times of solitude to deepen my bond with You,
LORD, for You are my source of contentment. I pray to experience
Your presence in these moments more than ever.

Thank you for carrying my burdens and reminding me that I am
never alone.

Amen.

Time with GOD

A kind gesture can go a long way. Do at least three random acts of kindness this week. Serve as a reminder that GOD's goodness can be found anywhere.

....

....

....

....

....

....

....

....

....

....

....

....

....

Week 46: Comparison & Condemnation

But if you have bitter envy and self-seeking in your hearts, do not boast and lie against the truth. This wisdom does not descend from above, but is earthly, sensual, demonic. For where envy and self-seeking exist, confusion and every evil thing are there.

JAMES 3:14–16, NKJV

Dear Father,

Please forgive me if I have ever compared myself to others. Help me to resist these temptations and stay grounded in my security. Remind me that I am Your masterpiece.

LORD, if I shall ever harbor envy toward another individual, please enlighten me. Help me to pray for them instead.

May I never become too critical of myself or others. With my gaze lifted, I focus on serving my own unique calling.

Amen.

Time with GOD

Make a list of ten things that you love about yourself. Embrace them and thank GOD for His blessings!

....

....

....

....

....

....

....

....

....

....

....

....

....

Week 47: Rising above Negativity

"No weapon formed against you shall prosper, And every tongue which rises against you in judgment You shall condemn. This is the heritage of the servants of the LORD, And their righteousness is from Me," says the LORD.

ISAIAH 54:17, NKJV

Dear Father,

When I receive words of criticism or discouragement, I sing of Your strength. I lean not on the judgments of others, but on Your heavenly promises.

I pray that You keep my head lifted throughout all circumstances and protect me from those who wish to divert me from my goals.

I declare peace over those who speak down on me. May You heal them and soften their hearts.

Amen.

Time with GOD

GOD is greater than any obstacle. What are some excuses you're ready to let go of?

....

....

....

....

....

....

....

....

....

....

....

....

....

Week 48: Truth & Honesty

Therefore each of you must put off falsehood and speak truthfully to
your neighbor, for we are all members of one body.

EPHESIANS 4:25, NIV

Dear Father,

Teach me to always be truthful, even when the consequences
seem daunting. Forgive me for my past lies as I commit to a life
of honesty.

I pray to foster this virtue in all of my relationships. My thoughts,
words, and actions shall no longer bear falsehoods.

May I move forth to love my brothers and sisters with a genuine
heart.

Amen.

Time with GOD

What does "honesty" mean to you? On a scale of one to ten, how honest are you?

....

....

....

....

....

....

....

....

....

....

....

....

....

Week 49: Dependability

Therefore encourage one another and build one another up, just as you are doing.

1 THESSALONIANS 5:11, ESV

Dear Father,

I pray to be a faithful and dependable friend.

Lead me to treat others' needs as my own, and grant me a spirit of sincerity. May I help them carry their burdens in times of need and celebrate their joys in times of good fortune.

Use me to be a blessing in somebody's life.

Amen.

Time with GOD

Think of someone who has uplifted you recently. This week, send them a small gift or a heartfelt note to express your gratitude.

....

....

....

....

....

....

....

....

....

....

....

....

....

Week 50: A Heart of Generosity

Do nothing from rivalry or conceit, but in humility count others
more significant than yourselves. Let each of you look not only to his
own interests, but also to the interests of others.

PHILIPPIANS 2:3–4, ESV

Dear Father,

As Your disciple, I seek to reflect Your essence of kindness and
generosity. May You cleanse my heart of any selfishness and clothe
me with the spirit of giving.

Lead me to opportunities where I can extend Your grace to those
in need.

Allow my words and actions to be a clear representation of Your
goodness, LORD.

Amen.

Time with GOD

What philanthropic cause are you most passionate about? This week, make a donation or volunteer your time to a relevant non-profit organization.

Afterward, reflect on your experience. Thank GOD for opening up your heart and granting you the ability to do meaningful work.

....

....

....

....

....

....

....

....

....

....

....

....

Week 51: Christian Fellowship

And let us consider how to stir up one another to love and good
works, not neglecting to meet together, as is the habit of some,
but encouraging one another, and all the more as you see the Day
drawing near.

HEBREWS 10:24-25, ESV

Dear Father,

Thank You for the bond that I share with my Christian brothers
and sisters. May You continue to unite our community under Your
banner.

Allow us to uplift one another as we celebrate Your glory. Through
the power of worship, we join our hearts together.

Help us to do the things that are pleasing to You, GOD. In Your
name, I pray.

Amen.

Time with GOD

With a fellow Christian, take turns telling your favorite stories from the Bible. How are those teachings still relevant today? How do they personally apply to your lives?

....

....

....

....

....

....

....

....

....

....

....

....

....

Week 52: Proclaiming GOD's Glory

Oh, give thanks to the LORD! Call upon His name; Make known His deeds among the peoples! Sing to Him, sing psalms to Him; Talk of all His wondrous works!

1 CHRONICLES 16:8–9, NKJV

Dear Father,

May You empower me to share my testimony, for my blessings are a true reflection of Your goodness and mercy.

Allow me to encourage others to lead lives of faith. Remind me that I am worthy of preaching Your name, and grant me the righteousness to share Your word with full conviction.

LORD, I am eager to serve as Your vessel. Thank You for choosing me to deliver Your messages and open up the hearts of others.

Amen.

Time with GOD

What is your story about your commitment to Christianity? Share your testimony with your peers. Be open about your faith!

....

....

....

....

....

....

....

....

....

....

....

....

....